Americans All biographies are inspiring life stories about people of all races, creeds, and nationalities who have uniquely contributed to the American way of life. Highlights from each person's story develop his contributions in his special field — whether they be in the arts, industry, human rights, education, science and medicine, or sports.

Specific abilities, character, and accomplishments are emphasized. Often despite great odds, these famous people have attained success in their fields through the good use of ability, determination, and hard work. These fast-moving stories of real people will show the way to better understanding of the ingredients necessary for personal success.

Susan B. Anthony

PIONEER IN WOMAN'S RIGHTS

by Helen Stone Peterson

illustrated by Paul Frame

GARRARD PUBLISHING COMPANY
CHAMPAIGN, ILLINOIS   1971 96.0

For Arthur, Jr., and Dianne

Picture credits:

Bettmann Archive: pp. 20, 28, 87
Brown Brothers: p. 84
Culver Pictures: p. 63

Standard Book Number: 8116–4570–3

Library of Congress Catalog Card Number: 76-151991

Contents

1. Susan Helps

Twelve-year-old Susan B. Anthony was setting the table for supper at the end of a lovely spring day in 1832. Her face lighted with a smile when she heard her father enter the house. Then his voice reached her as he spoke to her mother.

"Sally Ann who tends the spools at the mill is sick. I don't know anyone who can take her place."

Mr. Anthony was the managing partner of a large cloth mill in Battenville, New York. Six years earlier the Anthonys had moved to this village from Adams, Massachusetts, where Susan was born.

Susan had often visited the mill and watched the machines weave cotton yarn into cloth. Now she ran to her father.

"I know Sally Ann's job and I'd like to take her place. Please let me, father."

A look of surprise came over Mr. Anthony's face. But he always encouraged his children to be independent, and he nodded his approval. "I believe it would be a useful experience," he said.

Mrs. Anthony gave a little gasp. "Don't you think Susan is too young to work in the mill?" she protested gently.

Mr. Anthony smiled at Susan. "Your mother and I will discuss this and give you our decision."

Susan went back to setting the table. Just then her ten-year-old sister Hannah came into the room with a dish of yellow butter. When Hannah learned that Susan might work in the mill, she ran to tell her father that she too wanted the job.

The Anthonys were a big family. Susan and Hannah had a younger sister, Mary, a younger brother, Daniel, and an older sister, Guelma. Later another brother, Merritt, would complete the family circle.

At supper Mr. Anthony talked to Susan and Hannah. "Your mother has agreed to let one of you tend the spools. You will draw straws for the job, and the winner must divide the wages with the loser."

Susan drew the longest straw—and won. For the next two weeks she worked in the mill from six o'clock in the morning until six at night. Then she spent all her share of the earnings to buy six blue china cups and saucers. She gave this present to her mother.

"Thank you, my dear." Mrs. Anthony

spoke quietly as she always did, but a pleased smile brightened her tired face and warmed Susan's heart.

Mrs. Anthony toiled from dawn to dark, and her daughters cheerfully assisted her. Susan, taking tiny stitches, skillfully mended stockings and hemmed towels. She baked golden loaves of bread and cooked delicious puddings.

In the spring of 1832 food had to be prepared in larger quantities than usual, for Mr. Anthony's brickmakers were taking their meals with the family. Susan's father had hired these men to make bricks for the new home he was building. The house the family now lived in was only one and a half stories high. The new house would be much bigger.

"We will have fifteen rooms and four fireplaces," Mr. Anthony told his family.

With great pleasure he described the handsome curving stairway he planned for the entrance hall.

"Oh, it will be a beautiful home," exclaimed Susan, her eyes sparkling.

As soon as the Anthonys were settled in their new home, they invited their friends and relatives to visit them. They came, calling out good wishes to the family and filling the fine rooms with laughter. Happily Susan and her sisters poured lemonade and passed plates of doughnuts and gingerbread.

Mr. Anthony was growing wealthy. He now owned a second cloth mill, a small one, in Hardscrabble, a few miles away. In addition, he and his partner had built some tenant houses and a store in Battenville. Over the store Mr. Anthony had started a private school because he wanted his children to be taught by better teachers than those at the village school. Other children were invited to attend.

Soon Mr. Anthony moved his school to a large, attractive room in the new house. This was the first Battenville classroom in which each pupil had a separate seat. Though the seats were only stools without backs, the children were delighted not to be crowded onto the usual benches.

Susan took a fancy to Mary Perkins who came there to teach for a while. Miss Perkins supplied the pupils with books that had pictures. Susan, who had never seen such beautiful school books before, eagerly turned the pages.

When the children grew tired of bending over their books, Miss Perkins led them in physical exercises. The pupils enjoyed this new break in the school day

and did all of the exercises with vigor.

The year Susan was fifteen, she became the teacher for small children who attended the school during the summer months. She taught there again the following summer. Then, shortly after her seventeenth birthday in February 1837, Susan left home for the first time. She went to teach the children of a family in a neighboring village.

That fall Susan was ready to go much farther from home. Mr. Anthony wanted his daughters, as well as his sons, to have more education than was available to them in his school. At this time the only college in the country that would admit women was Oberlin, in Ohio, but there were boarding schools where girls could take some advanced courses. Susan's sister Guelma was starting her second year in a

14

boarding school near Philadelphia. In November 1837 Susan went there too.

This school was run by a Quaker lady. It was natural that Mr. Anthony had chosen a Quaker school, for he and his children were Quakers. Mrs. Anthony was not, though she regularly attended Quaker meetings with her family.

Susan expected to be a student at the school for two years. But after she had been there only six months, her father arrived one day with bad news.

"Our business is ruined, and our large mill has failed," Mr. Anthony told his daughters.

Susan, seeing the despair on her father's face, could hardly keep from weeping. She knew that other cloth mills were failing. The nation was suffering the worst financial crash in its history.

"What are you going to do?" asked Susan brokenly.

"I don't know," her father replied.

"Oh, I shall help him," Susan vowed.

The girls returned home with their father. Before long, some men to whom Mr. Anthony owed money claimed the beautiful house. Everything in it was put up for sale—even Mr. and Mrs. Anthony's eyeglasses.

"What a nightmare for my father and mother," thought Susan.

To her joy a kind uncle arrived. He bought the things the family wanted most to keep and gave them back to the Anthonys.

The family then moved to Hardscrabble, later called Center Falls. Mr. Anthony still owned the small cloth mill there, though it was heavily in debt. Now he hoped to build up the mill and make it successful.

Susan started to teach again and gave her father every dollar she could spare. One year she taught in the local village school. Other years she taught in schools farther away. At vacation time she hurried home, for she loved to be with her family.

Susan and her sisters had fun with other young people in their neighborhood. On summer days, laughing and talking, they climbed into buggies and drove off to picnics. In the winter they went sleigh riding over the snowy roads, with sleigh bells jingling. The young men placed thick heated planks under the girls' feet to keep them warm.

More than one man asked Susan to marry him, but there was no one for whom she really cared enough. "I would only become a household drudge," Susan told herself, "or maybe a doll." She chuckled at that thought.

As the years went by, Susan's father continued to work hard. Still, he could not make a success of his small cloth mill. He thought he might do better as a farmer, so he and his wife decided to move to a farm in Rochester, New York.

Guelma and Hannah did not go with the family, since both were now married and had their own homes close to Center Falls. Daniel, working nearby, chose to stay at his job. But on a cold November day in 1845, Susan and the rest of her family boarded a barge at the eastern end of the Erie Canal. The horses on the towpath pulled, the barge jerked forward, and the Anthonys were on their way to Rochester.

2. "Yah! Yah! Bloomer!"

Susan helped her family settle into their farmhouse. Then in the spring she left to teach the girls' classes at Canajoharie Academy, an excellent school in eastern New York.

Susan was now making as much money as a woman teacher could make. Yet she was paid only a fraction of the salary a man received for the same work. A woman teacher was always paid less, simply because she was a woman. Susan had long resented this inequality.

After three years at the academy,

Even as a young woman, Susan was dedicated to the ideal of equality for all people.

Susan resigned. "I will not spend the rest of my life teaching school," she decided. "But what shall I do?" To this question Susan did not yet know the answer.

She went back to her family's home. Her father, having found the farm too small to provide a living, was starting in the insurance business. To give him more time for building up his new business,

Susan took over the management of the farm.

One day her father drove her in his buggy to call on his new friend Frederick Douglass, the former Negro slave, who lived in Rochester. Mr. Douglass was publishing a newspaper in which he kept demanding immediate freedom for the millions of Negro slaves in the South. Many Northerners hated him. Businessmen, who were making money by trading with Southerners, did not want trouble stirred up. At that time there were even preachers who thundered that the blacks were an inferior race, born to serve white people.

But the Anthonys believed it was wicked to hold men as property. Susan found that she had the same views on slavery as Frederick Douglass. From their first meeting, she and the Negro leader were friends.

The Douglass family often spent lively Sundays at the Anthony farmhouse. "Mr. Douglass always brought along his violin," Susan remembered. "He liked to play it and sing, and we were happy listening to him."

When antislavery lecturers were in that part of the state, Mr. Anthony also invited them to spend Sunday at the farm. Among these lecturers were a few women. As they talked in the Anthony home or spoke in a meeting hall, Susan listened with admiration. Usually women were not permitted to say anything before an audience, but now a few courageous ones were speaking out against slavery.

"Shame on you women! Your place is clearly in the home," cried ministers.

Newspapermen wrote angrily, "Women do not belong in public life."

Susan became so interested in anti-slavery lectures that she sometimes went out of town to hear them. In May 1851 Susan, now thirty-one, went to an anti-slavery meeting in Seneca Falls near Rochester. As she and a friend walked along a street of that village, they unexpectedly met Elizabeth Cady Stanton. The friend introduced Susan to Mrs. Stanton.

"I have longed to meet you," said Susan, a warm smile sweeping over her rather plain face. Mrs. Stanton, a brilliant woman, was short and plump, with twinkling eyes and beautiful curly hair.

Susan knew that here at Seneca Falls in 1848, Mrs. Stanton and her Quaker friend Lucretia Mott had called the world's first convention for woman's rights. The women had drawn up a document protesting that they were being treated as if they were inferior to men. Mrs. Stanton had dared to go so far as to demand the right to vote, or suffrage, for women.

Before leaving Seneca Falls Susan called on Mrs. Stanton, and they had a long talk. "Remember the injustices to women as well as to the slaves," urged Mrs. Stanton. "A husband, no matter how worthless, is sole guardian of his children and can even give them away in his will. Every penny that a wife earns belongs to her husband." Mrs. Stanton went on to explain more injustices suffered by women.

"I tell you," she exclaimed, "there is mighty work to be done to lift woman to her proper place."

"She will be in her proper place when she has equal rights with men," answered

Susan thoughtfully. "I believe in equal rights for all regardless of sex or color."

Mrs. Stanton, nodding in agreement, added firmly, "The most important right is the vote. When we have the right to vote, we can change laws." After Susan returned to Rochester, she began to think hard about the importance of the right to vote.

A few weeks later she was invited back to Seneca Falls by Mrs. Stanton. This time Susan met Lucy Stone, the eloquent speaker from Massachusetts. Since Mrs. Stanton was busy raising a large family, Lucy Stone became the leader in organizing a national convention every year.

"It is wrong that we women are governed by laws in which we have no voice," Lucy said to Susan as they sat together in Mrs. Stanton's parlor. "We must fight for voting rights." Though Lucy was very small, weighing only about 100 pounds, she was full of courage, and her bright eyes flashed with determination.

The next year Susan attended her first woman's rights convention. Soon she reached an important decision. "What shall I do?" she had asked herself when she gave up teaching. At last she knew the answer to this question.

"I shall work for equal rights for all," she decided, "and my goal will be to win for women the right to vote." Susan felt confident that she would find a way to support herself. She had some savings and she had the backing of her father, who agreed with her decision wholeheartedly.

Now Susan took an unusual step. She put on the comfortable bloomer costume that had been designed by Elizabeth Miller, a cousin of Mrs. Stanton. It consisted of a loose dress that came a little below the knees and trousers that were gathered at the ankles. In this outfit women were no longer tightly laced at the waist, nor weighed down with pounds of long petticoats. The costume was named after Amelia Bloomer, who publicized it in a paper she edited at Seneca Falls.

"Yah! Yah! Bloomer!" Boys made fun of Susan when she walked along the street. They jeered at all women who appeared in the new style.

Once Susan and Lucy Stone wore their bloomers to New York City where they attended a meeting. As they walked away from the meeting, they noticed that they were being pursued by a group of boys. Susan and Lucy moved quickly, but the boys moved even faster. They completely

Some women wore their bloomer outfits in public, regardless of stares and jibes.

surrounded the two women and held them prisoner. Lots of people stopped to enjoy the sight, while the boys shouted:

Gibbery, gibbery gab
The women had a confab
And demanded the rights
To wear the tights
Gibbery, gibbery gab.

Susan and Lucy stood facing each other, helpless. Just then, a man who knew them both pushed through the crowd. With the aid of a policeman, he led the women to his carriage.

Susan continued to wear the bloomer costume for a while, but then gave it up.

"The costume attracted too much unfavorable attention," Susan told friends. "It was hurting the woman's rights movement." With a laugh she added, "I hope our other reforms will be more successful."

3. "The Ladies Always Have the Best Places"

Most newspapers were hostile to the woman's rights movement. "What are the rights which women seek?" scoffed the New York *Sun*. "The right to do wrong!"

Reporters ridiculed the women's meetings, calling them "tomfoolery conventions." They made fun of the speeches there. "Gabble," wrote reporters. "Silly rant."

"The whole world is against us," cried many women reformers. "How can we begin changing the status of women?"

"We can demand new laws from our state legislatures," proposed Susan, who had assumed the leadership in New York.

30

She drew up a petition that requested new laws to bring three reforms for women: the right to vote, the right of married women to control their earnings, and the right to have equal guardianship of their children. At this time the establishment of voting rights, along with these other rights, was left to the individual states.

To circulate the petition throughout New York, Susan enlisted women who wanted these changes. All the women, like Susan, were volunteer workers in different parts of the state. Susan herself canvassed the Rochester area.

In the cold winter of 1854, Susan tramped through the snow from house to house and asked for signatures on the petition. Many a housewife slammed the door in her face, snapping, "I have all the rights I want. Thank Heaven, I have a husband to look after me."

Yet in two months the faithful workers collected a total of 10,000 signatures. After Susan presented the signed petition to the legislature in Albany, Mrs. Stanton was allowed to address the lawmakers. She was the first woman to speak before the legislature. With pride Susan listened to her friend's scholarly plea for woman's rights. But the legislature refused to enact the requested laws.

"We shall keep coming back here until we get positive action," Susan warned the lawmakers.

The next year Susan traveled alone from one isolated village to another throughout the state. She lectured on woman's rights and asked for more signatures on the same petition. This long tour took courage.

So unpopular was the women's movement that in one town Susan was denied
the use of the meeting halls. The hotel
owner came to her rescue and turned his
dining room into a meeting room. In some
towns there was no way for Susan to
announce her lecture except by notices
that she handed out or nailed up in
conspicuous spots.

To cover her expenses, she charged an admission fee of twenty-five cents to the meetings. In Canandaigua thirteen-year-old Caroline Richards, who lived with her grandmother, went to hear Susan. This is what the schoolgirl wrote in her diary:

> Susan B. Anthony . . . talked very plainly about our rights and how we ought to stand up for them, and said the world would never go right until the women had just as much right to vote and rule as the men. . . . I could not make Grandmother agree with her at all and she said we might better all of us stayed at home.

At the end of her tour in 1855 Susan presented the petition to the legislature, but the lawmakers still did nothing. She patiently went back to lecturing and enrolling more names. In 1856 after she delivered the petition to the legislature, a committee wrote a report. As the chairman read it to the lawmakers, they burst into laughter.

> . . . The ladies always have the best places and choicest tidbit at the table. They have the best seats in the [railroad] cars, carriages, and sleighs; the warmest place in winter and the coolest in summer. . . . If there is any inequality . . . the gentlemen are the sufferers.

"How dare they make fun of all our hard work!" flared Susan, reading the story in the Albany *Register*. But her indignation quickly passed, leaving room only for her determination to persist in bringing pressure on the lawmakers.

Among other things, Susan took the initiative in arranging a woman's rights convention at Albany each year while the legislature was in session. Women came from every corner of the state, bringing to the lawmakers more signatures on their petition.

In 1860 the legislature finally acted. Women did not get the right to vote. But the lawmakers passed a bill that gave to married women the control of their earnings and equal guardianship of their children.

"We have won a great victory!" Susan joyfully told her co-workers. Woman's rights legislation, like that enacted in New York, spread from state to state.

4. Free the Slaves

By this time Susan was also working for the American Anti-Slavery Society at a salary of ten dollars a week. The society, recognizing her leadership ability, had asked Susan to take charge of its work in New York State.

"I welcome this opportunity," Susan told her family. Like all the Anthonys she regarded Negro slavery as evil, and she wanted to do something about it.

Slavery was becoming a burning national issue. Americans were divided as to whether it should be extended to the

ROOMS
FOR
RENT

new states entering the Union. Only a minority took the position of the Anti-Slavery Society, which demanded: "Free the slaves now!"

Susan threw herself into the work of planning schedules for the society's lecturers, who traveled in groups throughout the state. She always accompanied one of the groups. While traveling with an able Negro man and his sister, Susan ran into bitter racial hate. In some communities no hotel or boardinghouse would take in her two black friends.

"What lack of Christianity!" protested Susan. Blazing with anger, she would hunt until she found a private home where they could stay.

Susan knew that in many churches Negro families had to sit in pews apart from white people. Moreover, most of the state's public schools had separate classes for Negro children. In her lectures Susan lashed out at this discrimination.

"Here in the North Negroes are barred from many hotels, restaurants, churches, and schools. They are shut out from all but the most unskilled jobs."

"What do you want us to do with the blacks?" a hostile listener would ask.

Susan was always quick with her reply. "Treat the Negroes with equality and justice."

Flaming with fierce indignation over school segregation, Susan took time to attend a state teachers' convention where she introduced a long resolution that started this way: "Resolved: that the exclusion of colored youth from our public schools, academies, colleges, and universities is the result of wicked prejudice. . . ."

40

The convention broke into an uproar, and the teachers refused to approve the resolution. Instead, they adopted this statement: "The colored children of the state should enjoy equal advantages of education with the white."

In the winter of 1861, before the inauguration of the new president, Abe Lincoln, Susan met a group of antislavery speakers in western New York where they began a tour across the state. They found excitement at a high pitch, for southern states were seceding. Many Northerners truly were horrified at this breaking up of the Union.

Some of them thundered, "Don't let antislavery speakers be heard! Their agitation is the cause of all our troubles."

In Buffalo where Susan and the group were to speak, rioters rushed into the hall.

They shouted, stamped, and whistled, so that it was impossible for the lecturers to be heard.

Attacks on the antislavery movement spread elsewhere. At Port Byron, where Susan was presiding over a meeting, rowdies threw a large quantity of red pepper on the hot stove in the hall. Everyone fled from the suffocating fumes. In Syracuse, as soon as Susan and the other speakers stepped onto the platform, rotten eggs were thrown at them. Rough-looking men with pistols in their pockets surged toward the platform, shouting, "Throw them out!" Friends escorted the group quickly through a rear door. That night a hideous effigy labeled *Susan B. Anthony* was burned in the public square, while a drunken crowd screamed.

"Call off the rest of your meetings," a

friend pleaded with Susan. "The danger of violence is too great."

"No," replied Susan, her courage unwavering. "Freedom of speech is one of our most important American rights, and it's our duty to uphold it."

Yet only in Albany, the last stop on the tour, were the brave lecturers heard. There the mayor placed policemen in the audience, and he himself sat on the speakers' platform with a loaded gun across his knee.

In April cannons at Charleston, South Carolina fired on Fort Sumter, occupied by Union soldiers. The tragic Civil War had begun.

5. Amendments to the Constitution

Susan's beloved father died in November 1862 after a brief illness. For weeks Susan was desolate. Then she pulled herself together. "I will go forward," she resolved, knowing this is what her father would have wanted. He had always encouraged her to keep working towards equal rights for all.

Susan went to visit the Stantons in New York City, where they now lived. With the outbreak of the Civil War, the drive for woman's rights had come to a halt. Instead, women were making bandages for the wounded, nursing in hospitals, and working in factories and on farms in place of men who had gone to war.

"What can we do for our country?" Susan and Mrs. Stanton asked each other.

They soon found the answer. The Emancipation Proclamation, recently issued by President Lincoln, had freed the slaves in the rebellious states. But, if slavery was to be forever prohibited in the United States, emancipation must be written into the Constitution by means of an amendment. Charles Sumner, the Republican senator from Massachusetts, was pressing for this amendment, but a majority of the members of Congress were not ready to vote for it. They had to be convinced that public opinion supported the amendment.

Susan and Mrs. Stanton organized the Women's National Loyal League, which would circulate petitions demanding that

Congress pass the amendment. Susan became the league's paid worker, putting in long hours at her tiny office in New York.

"I go to a restaurant nearby for lunch," she wrote to her mother in the summer of 1863. "I always take strawberries with two tea rusks."

Susan mailed petitions to women from Maine to California. As signed petitions flowed back to her office, Mrs. Stanton's sons rolled them into huge bundles. Then they wrapped the bundles in yellow paper and tied them with red tape. On February 9, 1864 two strong men carried the bundles into the Senate and placed them on Senator Sumner's desk.

"You are doing a noble work," the senator wrote to the league. "Send on the petitions as fast as received."

By summer the league had sent petitions bearing almost 400,000 signatures, the largest number of names that had ever been collected in the United States for a single objective. This achievement helped convince Congress that public opinion supported the Thirteenth Amendment, which was now moving toward passage. The league disbanded.

The next year Susan made a long visit to her brothers Daniel and Merritt in Kansas where they now lived. Here, soon after the end of the war, Susan read in a newspaper the text of the proposed Fourteenth Amendment. It would extend citizenship and the vote to Negroes. But Susan was shocked to see the word "male" used three times to define voters. That word had never before appeared in the Constitution.

"If the word 'male' is written into the Constitution, it will be a new roadblock between women and the vote," thought Susan in alarm. "Now is the time for both Negroes and women to get the vote."

Ending her visit at once, Susan hastened to New York. She found Mrs. Stanton half frantic with concern over the possible introduction of the word "male" into the Constitution.

Together they wrote a petition that demanded the vote for women. Then they mailed copies to workers in the women's movement, along with letters requesting that the petition be signed and sent to Congress. To Susan's dismay, her friend Senator Sumner was not pleased with the avalanche of petitions that poured into his office.

"These petitions are untimely and

inopportune," he told the Senate. The Republican party, which was in power, refused to champion the vote for women. Intent on getting the votes of black men in the South, Republicans were determined to fight only for male Negro suffrage.

Confidently Susan turned for support to the antislavery men by whose side women had worked long and hard to free the slaves. She was bitterly disappointed when these men now turned their backs on woman suffrage. Wendell Phillips, president of the Anti-Slavery Society, said, "This is the Negro's hour. Do not clog his way."

The Fourteenth Amendment became part of the Constitution. It was followed by the Fifteenth Amendment that further protected the Negroes' right to vote.

Susan thought about the future of the Negro in America, and she spoke gravely to Mrs. Stanton.

"The white people must be educated to share their privileges with the blacks. And little children must be taught about human rights with the same exactness they are now taught the multiplication table. It is far more important for them to understand that all men are created equal, than to know that two times two equals four."

Susan's kind, honest face took on a look of iron determination. "As for me, my work will not be done until the power of the ballot is in the hands of all women—black and white."

6. Campaigning in Kansas

In 1867 Kansas submitted to voters an amendment to the state constitution that would give the ballot to women. For the first time in the United States, woman suffrage was being put to the vote.

"Send your strongest speakers to canvass this state for the amendment," a Republican state senator wrote to Susan. He knew that she was a leader in the suffrage movement.

"How I would rejoice to have one state where women might cast their ballots as naturally as their husbands do," thought Susan, filled with hope.

She persuaded Lucy Stone to spend the spring months in Kansas, speaking for the amendment. By September Susan and Mrs. Stanton had gone to the state. Susan, establishing headquarters in Lawrence, was the campaign manager.

Mrs. Stanton started over the prairie trails on a long, hard speaking tour. The strong mules pulling her carriage wore themselves out and had to be replaced by Indian ponies.

Three members of the well-known Hutchinson family, the most popular singing group in the North, came to help. They traveled through Kansas in their own carriage, drawn by two white horses.

With them Susan sent Reverend Olympia Brown, a talented woman minister who had come all the way from New England to help. Reverend Brown would speak briefly at meetings, urging passage of the amendment. Then the Hutchinsons would start singing:

Who votes for woman suffrage now will add new laurels to his brow.

Though many people did their very best for the campaign, Susan saw that the amendment was in great danger. She had counted on the Republican party to sponsor it. But the party in Kansas was split, and the most powerful group now actively opposed giving the ballot to women.

Susan was heartsick. "Where can we get support?" she asked herself.

Suddenly a telegram arrived from wealthy George Francis Train who offered to come and win Democratic votes for the amendment. Susan consulted Mrs. Stanton and other workers. All knew that Mr.

Train was eccentric, for he often said and did absurd things. But they knew also that they needed help desperately. They accepted his offer.

Lucy Stone denounced Susan and Mrs. Stanton for linking George Train's name to the cause. She and some other people in the East considered him "crack-brained."

Nevertheless, Susan accompanied Mr. Train on his campaign through Kansas. On the platform he was a showman, wearing lavender kid gloves and shiny patent leather boots.

One day, while driving to a meeting, Mr. Train asked Susan, "Why don't you women have your own newspaper?"

"Lack of money," replied Susan grimly. She had longed to have a paper through which she could educate public opinion on woman's right to vote.

"Well, I will give you the money," said Mr. Train. Susan did not believe he was serious. But that evening, as soon as Mr. Train stepped onto the platform, he made an announcement:

"When Miss Anthony gets back to New York City, she is going to start a woman suffrage paper. It will be called *The Revolution*. She will be the owner." He named Mrs. Stanton as one editor and Parker Pillsbury, a loyal friend of both women, as the second editor.

Meanwhile, on election day the amendment that would have given the ballot to women in Kansas was defeated, receiving 9,000 votes out of a total of 30,000. However, Susan was not discouraged. She told Mrs. Stanton, "Nine thousand forward-looking men voted for woman suffrage. I believe our drive is gaining."

7. *The Revolution*

The first issue of *The Revolution* was on the newstands in New York City on January 8, 1868. It was a handsome paper, a little smaller than today's tabloids. With pride Susan mailed 10,000 copies across the land.

"Let women demand the right to vote in thunder terms," urged *The Revolution*.

Soon a crushing burden fell upon Susan. Assuring her that he would send money for the paper, Mr. Train departed for Great Britain. There he spoke out for Irishmen who wanted their country freed from Great Britain. The British government arrested Mr. Train and sentenced him to prison. After a short time no more funds came for *The Revolution.*

Susan began to borrow money to keep the weekly paper going. She worked day and night to secure subscriptions for it. Her efforts took her to Washington, D.C. She even went to the White House to ask President Andrew Johnson to add his name to the paper's subscription list. *The Revolution* carried an account of her visit there:

"I waited two hours in the anteroom among huge half-bushel-measure spittoons and terrible filth . . . where the smell of tobacco . . . was powerful," reported Susan.

When Susan did at last see the president, he said that he didn't want the paper. "I have a thousand such applications everyday," he explained a little wearily.

"Mr. President, you are mistaken. You never had an application like this in your life," replied Susan bluntly. She talked about woman's right to the ballot and warned that her paper would keep hammering away until women got their rights.

"That brought him to his pocketbook," reported Susan. "He signed his name *Andrew Johnson* with a bold hand, as much as to say, 'Anything to get rid of this woman.'"

While Susan went about the business of publishing her paper, she became concerned over the problems of working women. Having entered the labor market during the Civil War, women were working in increasing numbers. Susan invited them to a meeting in the office of *The Revolution*.

They came—careworn seamstresses, milliners, clerks, factory workers, and typesetters. All these workers put in ten to fourteen hours a day and some of them earned as little as four dollars a week.

"Girls, listen to me," urged Susan. "You must not work for these starving prices any longer. Have a spirit of independence!"

She helped them organize a Working Women's Association that aimed at improving conditions. It was deeply satisfying to Susan when the typesetters, with her aid, went on to organize their own union. This was one of the first women's unions in the United States.

"Stick to this union, girls," advised Susan earnestly. "Together say 'Equal pay for equal work.'"

The Revolution fearlessly reported the problems of working women and news of their organization. But this coverage stirred up criticism of the paper because the subject was unpopular with conservative people.

The Revolution called for many reforms, including more liberal divorce laws. Since there was opposition to divorce for any reason, the paper's liberal ideas again offended conservative people. Lucy Stone was outraged that the question was brought up in a suffragists' paper.

In May 1869 Susan and Mrs. Stanton decided that the time had come to have a new, nationwide organization with the sole purpose of winning the vote for women. Under their leadership the National Woman Suffrage Association was formed.

This old print illustrates a meeting of the National Woman Suffrage Association.

Lucy Stone and her followers in New England did not join. For them *The Revolution* was too liberal, and they had never forgiven Susan and Mrs. Stanton for associating with Mr. Train. In November 1869 Lucy led in founding a rival organization, the American Woman Suffrage Association.

On January 8, 1870, exactly two years after the first issue of *The Revolution,* Lucy and her friends began publishing a suffrage paper, known as the *Woman's Journal.* It had financial backing and conservative editors who did not scare away influential people.

The field was not large enough to support two papers, and *The Revolution* lost out. Susan loved her paper. When she had to give it up in May 1870, her heart almost broke.

"It was like signing my own death warrant," Susan wrote in her diary with anguish.

She personally assumed *The Revolution's* staggering debt of $10,000. Bravely Susan promised, "I will work with might and main to pay every dollar of this honest debt."

8. Susan Votes

After Susan gave up *The Revolution,*
she went to work as a lecturer.

By this time, women who were good
speakers were in great demand. Many
people preferred to go to an auditorium
to listen to an interesting speaker rather
than stay at home and read. All over the
country large audiences turned out to
hear Susan plead for woman's right to
vote.

But many newspapers called her a
mischief-maker. And they sneered at her
appearance, describing her as an angular,

sour old maid. "If all woman's righters look like that, the theory will lose ground . . . ," wrote the Detroit *Free Press* in an insulting article.

Bearing herself with dignity, Susan paid no attention to the jibes. Many people in her audiences liked her appearance. "She is an intelligent-looking woman," they remarked. They saw too that she was tastefully dressed. On the platform Susan always wore a dark silk gown with a collar of white lace.

She earned good fees for her lectures. By 1872 she had reduced the debt of *The Revolution* by several thousand dollars.

Susan was now considering woman suffrage from a new angle. Some lawyers claimed that women who were citizens of the United States already had the right to vote under the Fourteenth Amendment.

These lawyers said, "The vote is a privilege of citizenship."

"I shall test this possibility," decided Susan as the national election of 1872 drew close.

On November 1 she was in Rochester, where her sisters Guelma and Hannah now lived with their families. Susan asked them and her sister Mary to go with her to register as voters. At the shoemaker's shop, which was the place for registering, the four sisters requested the election inspectors to enroll them.

"What do you say?" one inspector asked another.

"I say it's unlawful," came the reply.

"And I say it is your duty!" declared Susan. After an hour-long discussion with the inspectors, she persuaded them to register her as well as her three sisters.

Then Susan rushed to the homes of friends in her part of the city, urging all the women to register.

On election day, November 5, 1872, Susan triumphantly entered her polling place and voted. Fourteen other women also voted there.

Two weeks later a United States marshal rang Susan's doorbell. "I have a warrant for your arrest," he told Susan. "You are charged with voting without a lawful right."

Susan's trial opened on June 17, 1873 in a crowded courtroom at Canandaigua, New York. Susan studied the prim-looking judge, Ward Hunt, and the all-male jury. "A man's world here," she thought. "Can a woman get justice?"

Susan's lawyer, Mr. Henry Selden of Rochester, made a masterly presentation of her case. Then the district attorney argued for the government.

When he finished, Susan was shocked to see Judge Hunt pull from his pocket a paper he had written before hearing the evidence. Now he read it aloud. In this prepared opinion the judge held that the question was one of law, and he directed the jury to find Susan guilty.

Mr. Selden jumped to his feet. "I ask your Honor to submit this case to the jury."

Ignoring Mr. Selden, the judge ordered the clerk to record the verdict. "Gentlemen of the jury," recited the clerk, ". . . you say you find the defendant guilty. . . ."

The jurors looked dazed. They had not said a single word.

Again Mr. Selden jumped to his feet. "Poll the jury!"

"No," ruled the high-handed judge. And to the jury he said, "Gentlemen of the jury, you are discharged."

The next day Susan returned to the courtroom for sentencing. Judge Hunt ordered her to stand up and then asked, "Have you anything to say?"

"Yes, your Honor, I have many things to say," retorted Susan. "You have trampled underfoot every vital principle of our government. . . ."

The judge tried to hush her, asserting that he could not listen to her arguments any longer.

Susan persisted in listing the rights that had been denied to her: "Your denial of my citizen's right to vote . . . , the denial of my right to a trial by a jury . . ."

"Sit down!" ordered the judge.

But Susan continued until she finished

what she wanted to say about injustices. Then she sat down.

"Stand up!" ordered the judge. He pronounced her sentence, a fine of one hundred dollars. She would also have to pay the cost of the trial.

"Your Honor, I shall never pay a dollar of your unjust penalty," declared Susan. And she never did.

But the judge did not order her to prison for failure to pay. He knew that if Susan were imprisoned, she could appeal to a higher court. The government dropped its case against the other women who had voted with Susan.

Another test case, however, was traveling up through the courts. In 1875 the Supreme Court handed down the decision that women could not vote under the Fourteenth Amendment.

"Doesn't this decision discourage you?" a reporter asked Susan.

"Never!" she shot back. "I shall work without ceasing for an amendment that gives the ballot to women."

9. The Nation's Hundredth Birthday

Susan continued her strenuous lecture tours back and forth across the country. No one ever heard her complain, but she looked tired and worn.

At last there came a wonderful day. On May 1, 1876 Susan's blue eyes were shining as she wrote in her diary: "I have paid the last dollar of *The Revolution* debt!"

Later in the month Susan hurried to bustling Philadelphia. It was America's Centennial year, the hundredth birthday of the founding of the nation in 1776. In celebration a huge exposition was to be held at Philadelphia during the summer. Susan saw that the exposition offered women a golden opportunity to focus attention on their right to vote and on the need for a woman suffrage amendment to the Constitution.

Mrs. Stanton and other leaders in the National Woman Suffrage Association joined Susan in Philadelphia. Together the leaders wrote a *Declaration of Rights for Women*. Susan asked permission to present this declaration at the large meeting planned for the Fourth of July in Independence Square.

"No," replied General Joseph Hawley, chairman of the Centennial commission. "We propose to celebrate what we have done in the last hundred years, not what we have failed to do."

Then these suffrage leaders decided that

it would be fitting for a woman from each state to sit on the big platform, alongside all the men who would sit there. They asked for seats for the women.

"Impossible!" replied General Hawley. "The platform is already crowded."

At the denial of these requests, Susan and her co-workers rebelled. "We *shall* leave one bright remembrance for the women of the next centennial," they vowed. "The daughters of 1976 will know that the women of 1876 asserted their right to equality."

They made plans for confrontation and action.

Susan succeeded in obtaining several admission tickets to the platform. On the Fourth of July she and three co-workers took seats there. They listened while a man read the Declaration of Independence.

76

When he was finished, the audience rose.

"Now!" Susan directed her followers.

The women marched forward. Thrusting a rolled parchment scroll into the hands of the presiding official, Susan said, "I present to you a *Declaration of Rights* from the women citizens of the United States."

The official's face went white, but he bowed and said nothing.

The women walked out of the meeting, handing to the left and right copies of their declaration. Men stretched out their hands for the paper. Others, farther away, stood on their seats and shouted that they wanted copies.

"Order!" boomed General Hawley. The General, having been busy with some details, had missed the beginning of this scene. But now his voice kept booming: "Order! Order!"

After the Centennial, Susan embarked on a campaign to compel Congressional action on a woman suffrage amendment. She urged the American Woman Suffrage Association to join in this effort. Its leaders, though, preferred to work for the vote in individual states, as Lucy Stone,

Susan, and Mrs. Stanton had done in Kansas. The National Association cooperated in state campaigns, but it insisted that the best way of winning suffrage was by an amendment to the Constitution.

The National Association, having grown in the seven years since its origin, now had members across the nation. Susan asked them to collect signatures on petitions for the proposed amendment. The women brought the signed petitions to Washington, D.C. when they came for their annual convention in January 1877.

One afternoon, just as members of the House of Representatives were finishing their day's work, Susan led a group of women into their chamber. To each representative the women handed petitions from his own state.

The next day Susan led the group to

the Senate. After the women presented their petitions, they seated themselves in the gallery to watch what would happen. Most senators, reading the petitions, grinned or laughed. When one sarcastically recommended that all the petitions be given to the Committee on Public Lands, the majority of the senators voted for this.

Since such a committee could do nothing for woman suffrage, Susan was angered. She went back to the convention and cried out to the women, "When you return home, get thousands of additional signatures on petitions. Keep sending them to Congress!"

And that is what the women did.

A year later, on January 10, 1878, the Honorable Aaron Sargent of California stood up in the Senate. Senator Sargent, who was Susan's close friend, introduced a proposal for a Sixteenth Amendment to the Constitution. The text was simple, using the language of the Fifteenth Amendment.

"The right of citizens of the United States to vote shall not be denied or abridged by the United States or by any State on account of sex."

This measure was received with respect and was referred to the proper committee. But after considering the proposed amendment the committee turned it down.

10. Going Forward

Every winter Susan spent some time in Washington. She lobbied at the Capitol, pleading for support for the woman suffrage amendment. She sorely missed Senator Sargent who was not reelected, but she made new friends in both the Senate and the House.

Susan went to these men at the beginning of each new term of Congress and appealed to them to reintroduce the amendment. When she could not find a senator or representative in his office, she searched him out at his home.

"I thought just as likely as not you would come fussing around . . . ," her good friend Senator Henry Blair of New Hampshire wrote to her one winter when she was pushing him for action. "I wish you would go home. . . . Go off and get married!"

The amendment was reintroduced in Congress again and again. In each chamber it was regularly referred to a committee. Susan persuaded the committees to hold hearings at the time of the annual convention of the National Woman Suffrage Association in Washington. Then she took the best speakers, including Mrs. Stanton, to address the committees.

One year, instead of the usual speakers, Susan took some of the fine young women she was now recruiting into the association. The Senate committee listened to them courteously, but after the hearing one senator spoke to Susan.

"Where are the old war horses? We want to hear those strong-minded women."

When Mrs. Stanton learned of this remark, she laughed heartily. And she said to Susan, "Well, you and I never sat like little birds on a limb singing, 'Suffrage, if you please.'"

A leader in the woman's rights movement addresses a congressional committee and her fellow suffragists at the Capitol.

The next day Mrs. Stanton and other long-time workers addressed the Senate committee.

Despite all these efforts, however, only once during the 1880's did the amendment advance from committee to a vote by the entire Senate. There it was hotly opposed and defeated. In the House during these same years, the amendment did not even once come up for a vote.

When Susan was sixty-three years old, she took the first real vacation of her life. One of the young workers persuaded Susan to accompany her to Europe as a companion, with expenses paid. Susan had a delightful time. And in England she talked with women who were also trying to win the right to vote in their country.

"How splendid it would be if women from many nations could gather together

for an international conference," said
Susan, a little breathless at the thought.
Her new English friends liked the idea.

The large international conference was
held in March 1888 at Washington, D.C.
under the auspices of the National
Woman Suffrage Association. Delegates
came from Europe and Asia. Lucy Stone
and other members of the American
Woman Suffrage Association also attended.
For the first time women from all parts
of the world discussed their movement for
equality.

Newspapers praised the conference
highly. "What a change!" thought Susan.
"I remember when the press had only
ridicule for women's meetings."

Newspapers had high praise too for
Susan, who presided at the meetings.
Again Susan thought, "What a change!"

Elderly Susan B. Anthony sits at a desk
cluttered with papers and mementos of a
lifetime devoted to woman's rights.

She remembered when she was the laugh-
ingstock of the press.

Young members in both the National
and American Associations enjoyed seeing
the three pioneers together—Susan,
Mrs. Stanton, and Lucy Stone. "Let us
unite," pleaded the young people. "Both
organizations have the same goal—votes
for women."

Susan welcomed the union. Details were worked out, and in 1890 the two organizations merged under the name of the National American Woman Suffrage Association. Susan wanted Mrs. Stanton to be the first president.

"It is only right," she told the members. "Long ago at Seneca Falls she was the first woman in this nation to demand the vote for women." Mrs. Stanton was elected president of the unified, more powerful suffrage association.

Susan looked ahead with hope, telling herself, "Now women will give a strong pull and a pull all together for the vote."

11. President

In 1892 Susan was elected president of the united Woman Suffrage Association. Mrs. Stanton retired, and the following year Lucy Stone died.

When the nation prepared for the World's Fair at Chicago in 1893, Susan worked with influential leaders to make sure that women would have a prominent part. She herself attended and made numerous speeches. People now honored Susan as one of the nation's most distinguished citizens and crowded into auditoriums to hear her.

When some clergymen wanted the fair

closed on Sundays, Susan spoke her mind. She pointed out that it was the only day many working people could attend.

"Would you like to have a son of yours go to Buffalo Bill's Wild West Show on Sunday?" an indignant clergyman asked Susan.

"Certainly," she replied.

The delighted Buffalo Bill sent her tickets for one of his performances. Susan went, accompanied by a group of young women. When Buffalo Bill rode into the arena, he made straight for her seat. Reining his prancing horse in front of Susan, he swept off his hat in a grand salute. Laughing, Susan rose and waved her handkerchief at Buffalo Bill. The crowd broke into wild applause.

From the fair Susan traveled to her home in Rochester. She and her sister

Mary, a retired schoolteacher, now lived there together. Her other sisters and her mother were dead. Susan still kept in touch with her brothers in Kansas, and her nieces and nephews often visited the Rochester home.

Susan continued to work in states where woman suffrage came up for a vote. She had done this many times since that first campaign in Kansas, but there had been a series of defeats. Wyoming, in 1890, was the first state to give women the vote. During the 1890's victory came in three more states—Colorado, Idaho, and Utah.

Susan still kept pressure on Congress, for she held fast to her belief that votes for all women must come through a constitutional amendment. Susan resigned the presidency of the Woman Suffrage Association in 1900, when she was eighty years old. But she never stopped working for the amendment.

Addressing the association's national convention in February 1906, Susan said in a voice that was clear, though weak, "The fight must not cease! You must see that it does not stop!"

Instantly all the women were on their feet. For ten minutes they applauded and cheered their great pioneer leader. Many wept. They saw that Susan was very frail. As they looked upon her good face, now so pale, they felt that they were saying good-bye.

One month later Susan died. She was eighty-six years old.

Crusaders for the federal suffrage measure named it the Susan B. Anthony Amendment. It was passed in 1920, not as the Sixteenth Amendment for which

Susan had labored, but as the Nineteenth Amendment. Exactly one hundred years after Susan's birth, women throughout the United States at last had the right to vote.

"I believe in equal rights," Susan had said at the beginning of her long courageous struggle. After winning suffrage, women still did not have total equality with men. When women later took up the fight for this goal, they were trying to finish the work that Susan and other pioneers had begun.

Index